PREDICTIONS

Climate

ANDREW GOUDIE

PHŒNIX

A PHOENIX PAPERBACK

First published in Great Britain in 1997 by
Phoenix, a division of the Orion Publishing Group Ltd
Orion House
5 Upper Saint Martin's Lane
London, WC2H 9EA

A CIP catalogue record for this book is available
from the British Library.

ISBN 0 297 81929 1

Typeset by SetSystems Ltd, Saffron Walden
Set in 9/14 Stone Serif
Printed in Great Britain by
Clays Ltd St Ives plc

Contents

Introduction

In the second half of the nineteenth century and the early years of the twentieth there was a widely held view that human societies, human history and human traits were moulded by climatic conditions. There was a school of thought that was termed 'climate determinism'. Members of this school, which included the historian Henry Buckle and the geographer Arnold Guyot, believed that the differences they perceived in the level of civilization between temperate Europe and the warmer climes of lower latitudes could be ascribed to climatic influences. Guyot, for example, remarked: 'As there is a *temperate* hemisphere and a *tropical* hemisphere, we may in the same manner, say there is a *civilized* and a *barbarous* hemisphere.' He was clear about the value of a temperate climate: 'In the temperate climates all is activity, movement. The alternations of heat and cold, the changes of the seasons, a fresher and more bracing air, incite man to a constant struggle, to forethought, to the vigorous employment of all his faculties.' Conversely: 'the people of the tropical continents will always be the hands, the workmen, the sons of toil'.

Tropical peoples lacked what was sometimes called a

'climatic discipline'. Furthermore, some of the climatic determinists feared that the white races would degenerate in the tropics and become sexually depraved. Ellsworth Huntington, the Yale geographer and lapsed missionary, believed that vice was stimulated by high temperatures and the associated paucity of clothing, and in his book *Civilization and Climate* (1915) he described the Zulus (sic) of Northern Rhodesia thus:

> During the years when the young men ought to be getting new ideas and thinking out the many little projects and the few great ones which combine to cause progress, the vast majority are thinking of women and planning to gain possession of some new woman or girl. Under such circumstances no race can rise to any high position.

He also argued that climate was one of the reasons that helped greatly in explaining 'Why the Japanese fail to raise to European standards in orderliness, precision and mechanical accuracy'. One suspects that he might not take such a view today.

The climatic determinists, including that darling of London society, the émigré anarchist Prince Kropotkin, also believed that climate was a driving force in history and that fluctuations of climate could cause fluctuations in human affairs. They were particularly intrigued by the rise and fall of cultures and civilizations in the arid heartlands of Central Asia. But climatic determinism declined in popularity and esteem from the 1920s onwards, partly because of a distaste for its racial overtones, partly because of the sometimes crude way it had been applied to historical explanation, and partly because it was argued that as civilization proceeds humans become progressively divorced from the physical environment, of which climate is a part.

However, the decline of climatic determinism does not in itself mean that the need to assess the climatic factor in human affairs can be ignored. Indeed, particularly in France, there is a fine school of history that has interpreted some of the vicissitudes of European history in terms of its climatic history: the fortunes of the peoples of some alpine valleys from Norway to northern Italy were intimately tied up with the state of their glaciers; runs of cold years could render agriculture marginal in the uplands of Britain; a run of lean drought years could damage the grain lands around the Mediterranean; and the spread of sea ice could isolate settlements in Iceland and Greenland. There is evidence for all these tendencies in the history of Europe over the last thousand years.

Likewise, it would be foolish to assume that, as civilization has progressed and urbanization become more pervasive, humans have become progressively divorced from their physical environment. One can ask who is more dependent in the long run: the Australian Aboriginal, who must virtually learn to smell out the existence of water beneath the ground in order to survive and who moves with the rains; or the citizens of some great conurbations whose world would come crashing down if their sources of food and water were cut off and who probably could not survive in a parched wilderness for more than a few days? Nomadic pastoralists take out insurance against drought by mixing different types of stock, or by exchanging animals with kinsfolk in neighbouring areas. Inhabitants of modern cities, on the other hand, cope with the ever-growing property losses from flood and hurricane by claiming against Lloyd's of London. Both they and the financial sector are hugely vulnerable. The fact is that climate matters in the modern world and climate change matters even more.

The Past and the Present

The climate of the world is ever changing. It is invariable only in its variability. It has changed repeatedly and substantially throughout geological time and both before and during the presence of humans on the face of the earth. Changes have ranged from the essentially minor fluctuations within the period of instrumental record (with durations in the case of events like the Sahel Drought since the mid-1960s of the order of a decade or decades) to those of the most significant geological periods with durations of many millions of years. For example, over the last billion years there have been at least six major ice ages when great ice caps have enveloped substantial parts of the earth's surface. Such extensive phases of ice age activity appear to have been separated by millions of years of relative warmth when ice caps and glaciers have been largely absent.

The latest of these long periods of warmth saw the existence of the dinosaurs and the deposition of the Chalk of the Cretaceous seas. It extended into the early Tertiary (round about 40 to 60 millions years ago) when the North Atlantic region may have been characterized by a widespread, tropical moist forest type of vegetation. The London Clay, deposited in the Palaeocene, around 60 million years ago, contains the fossils of warmth-loving plants: palm, mangrove and Pandanus (screw pine). As recently as the Oligocene, around 30 million years ago, the climate of Britain was broadly comparable to that of a region like the south-eastern United States today.

Gradually, however, the world's climate began to cool during a phase called the Cainozoic Climate Decline. The causes of this decline are still not fully understood, but the trend seems to be associated with the movement of the earth's great tectonic plates and with the break-up of the ancient supercontinent of Pangaea into the individual continents we know today. Around 50 million years ago Antarctica separated from Australia and gradually shifted southwards into its present position centred over the South Pole. At the same time the continents of Eurasia and North America moved towards the North Pole. As more and more land became concentrated in high latitudes ice caps could develop. Their highly reflective surfaces bounced back a great deal of incoming heat from the sun, and as a consequence climate probably cooled all over the world. Ocean currents were at the same time transformed by such events as the opening up of the Atlantic Ocean as the continents drifted apart, while the circulation of the great wind belts was transformed by the uplift of the Himalayas and the Tibetan Plateau. Cold ocean waters, fed by a developing Antarctic ice cap, favoured the development of coastal deserts like the Atacama and the Namib, and about 2.4 million years ago glaciers developed in mid-latitudes and the latest ice-age period was initiated.

This latest ice age, which has characterized most of the time during which humans have inhabited the earth, did not consist of just one great spasm of cold. It was composed of multiple alternations of great cold (called glacials and stadials) with more equable stages of relatively greater warmth (interglacials and interstadials). In all, our studies of sediments retrieved from cores extracted from the ocean floors suggest that there have been no fewer than seventeen cycles of glacials and interglacials in the last 1.6 million years. In other words, each cycle of alternating cold and warmth has lasted about 100,000 years.

During the cold phases, the last of which peaked as recently as 18,000 years ago, the world was totally different in almost all respects from the one we know today. In North America the ice cap may have been 3,300 metres thick and it reached far south into the Ohio–Mississippi basin at latitude 39°N. In the British Isles ice covered much of Ireland and Wales and in the east reached the Norfolk coast. To the south of that there was a largely treeless tundra underlain by permanently frozen subsoil called permafrost. Other huge ice caps covered Scandinavia and the North European Plain, the Alps, Patagonia and much of western New Zealand.

Areas to the equatorwards of the great ice caps were

not unaffected by the great cooling. The cyclone-bearing westerlies brought rain to what are now the arid lands of the south-west United States, transforming the current Great Salt Lake into a freshwater body – Lake Bonneville – the size of present-day Lake Michigan. Conversely, because the oceans were cooler, the tropical circulation was weaker, causing the Sahara, the Thar and the Australian deserts, with their associated dune fields, to expand. Large tracts of what is now savanna were transformed into sand sea, and the great rainforests of Amazonia and the Congo (Zaire) Basin were fragmented. Even that great freshwater body, Lake Victoria, became salty.

Of no lesser significance for the state of the earth was that the retention of large volumes of water in the ice caps, which were around three times more extensive than today, led to a global fall of sea levels that may have exceeded 100 metres. Great expanses of continental shelf became dry land. The waters retreated from much of the Irish Sea, the North Sea, the English Channel, the Persian Gulf and the island-studded shelf between Asia and Australia.

After the glacial peak at 18,000 years ago, the world started to warm once more, and by about 10,000 years ago it had entered the phase of relative warmth called the Holocene interglacial in which we now live. However, the warming was not uninterrupted. Around 11,000 years ago, in a phase named the Younger Dryas, there was a time of suddenly renewed cold, which lasted perhaps for a thousand years and saw glaciers return to the British highlands. Indeed, the Holocene has not been climatically stable. There have been phases of relative warmth compared to today, together with periods of relative cold. The former is illustrated by a warm phase – the so-called 'altithermal' of the mid-Holocene about 6,000 years ago – and by the so-called Little Optimum of medieval times, when vineyards occurred as far north as York. The latter is characterized by the Little Ice Age, which occurred between the Middle Ages and the mid-nineteenth century. Glaciers expanded down-valley in the Alps and Scandinavia, harvests were cruelly poor in marginal areas like the Scottish Highlands, and the settlements that the Vikings had established in Greenland declined catastrophically.

Lower latitudes were not immune to these Holocene fluctuations. In the torrid dry heart of the Sahara Desert it has for long been suspected that climatic conditions were wetter at some stage or stages in the Holocene than they are at present. This was deduced from facts such as the widespread distribution of rock paintings, cattle-tethering stones, stone tools and pottery in areas which are currently far removed from waterholes. Certain of the species represented in central Saharan rock paintings, notably elephant, rhino, hippo and giraffe, were regarded as being representative of a moderately to strongly luxuriant savanna flora. Some pollen analyses have confirmed this story, as have radio-carbon dates on widespread lake and river deposits. Lake Chad was greatly expanded in depth and area and crocodile-infested rivers flowed eastwards from the Sahara into the Nile. In effect the Sahara did not exist during much of the early Holocene.

Climatic changes of considerable significance, albeit of relatively short duration, have also been typical of the twentieth century, though increasingly it becomes difficult to isolate the effects of natural climatic changes from those environmental changes caused by human-kind. In Southern Africa, for example, there is evidence for a number of quasi-periodic rainfall oscillations with an average period of about eighteen years. Since the turn of the century there have been eight approxi-mately nine-year spells of either predominantly above-average rainfall alternating with below-normal rainfall. On the south side of the Sahara a dry epoch of severe drought conditions started in the mid-1960s and con-tinued and intensified into the 1980s. The area of Lake Chad declined from 23,500 square kilometres in 1963 to about 2,000 in 1985, which is probably the lowest level of the century. Dust-storm frequencies in the Sahel and Sudan zones on the south side of the Sahara increased four to six times during that period as drought and humans depleted the vegetation cover and exposed the soil to wind attack. In the same vein one can refer to the Dust Bowl years of the 1930s in the High Plains of the USA, when 'black blizzards' of dust, comprised of valuable topsoil, caused great social distress. At places like Dodge City there were over 100 dust-storm days a year in the mid-1930s. This dust-storm era, the so-called 'Dirty Thirties', was a result of low rainfall, high temperatures, searing winds and human activities. The 'busting of the sod', caused by the increasing use of mechanized agriculture in response to increasing wheat prices after the First World War and the growing availability of the internal-combustion engine to power trucks and tractors, exposed the topsoil to wind attack.

Above all, the twentieth century has also been a time of general warming. Global mean surface air temperature has increased by between about 0.3 and 0.6°C, and the 1980s and 1990s have been especially warm decades. The ten warmest years in the last 130 have all occurred in those decades.

We have then, in the past and the present, a very clear picture that climate has seldom if ever been stable. Climate has changed repeatedly and substantially in all latitudes and at a range of different timescales. This is the case even without the intervention of human activities in the climatic system. There is thus no reason why natural climatic fluctuations should not happen in the future. The probability is that they will. The past and present tell us that in predicting future climates we must be aware of the natural mechanisms that drive the ever-changing earth. Any human-induced climate changes have to be seen against the background of this profound natural variability. Let us now consider what these natural driving forces are.

The Driving Forces
of Climate Change

No completely acceptable explanation of climatic change has ever been presented, and no one process acting alone can explain all scales of climatic change. The complexity of possibly causative factors involved is daunting.

The complexity becomes evident if we follow the pathway of radiation derived from the ultimate driving force of climate – the sun. First of all, for reasons such as the varying tidal pull being exerted on the sun by the planets, the quality and quantity of outputs of solar radiation may change. It has been recognized that the sun's radiation output changes both in quantity (through association with such familiar phenomena as sunspots, which are dark regions of lower surface temperature on the sun's surface) and in quality (through changes in the ultra-violet range of the solar spectrum). Cycles of solar activity have been established for the short term by many workers, with eleven- to twenty-two years cycles being particularly noted. Eighty- to ninety-year sunspot cycles have also been postulated. The observations of sunspots in historical times have also given a measure of solar activity and one very striking feature of the record is the near absence of sunspots between AD 1640 and 1710, a period sometimes called the Maunder Minimum. It is perhaps significant that this minimum occurred during some of the more extreme years of the rigorous Little Ice Age. Some evidence of possible longer-term solar effects comes from studies of the oscillation in the concentration of atmospheric ^{14}C (radiocarbon), which may in turn depend partly upon variations in the emission of solar radiation.

The receipt of such varying radiation at the earth's surface might itself vary because of the presence of fine interstellar matter (nebulae) through which the earth might from time to time pass, or which might interpose itself between the sun and our planet. This would tend to reduce the receipt of solar radiation. Likewise, the passage of the solar system through a dust lane bordering a spiral arm of the Milky Way galaxy might cause a temporary reduction in receipt of the sun's radiation output.

The receipt of incoming radiation will also be affected by the position and configuration of the earth. Such changes do take place, and there are three main astronomical factors which have been identified as of probable importance, with all three occurring in a cyclic manner. Firstly, the earth's orbit around the sun is not a perfect circle but an ellipse. If the orbit were a perfect circle then the summer and winter parts of the year would be equal in their length. With greater eccentricity the length of the seasons will display a greater difference. Over a period of about 96,000 years, the eccentricity of the earth's orbit can 'stretch' by departing much further from a circle and then revert to almost true circularity.

Secondly, changes take place in the 'precession of the equinoxes', which means that the time of year at which the earth is nearest the sun varies. The reason is that the earth wobbles like a child's top and swivels round its axis. This cycle has a periodicity of about 21,000 years.

Thirdly, changes occur, with a periodicity of about 40,000 years, in the 'obliquity of the ecliptic' – the angle between the plane of the earth's orbit and the plane of its rotational equator. This movement has been likened to the roll of a ship with tilt varying from 21° 39' to 24° 36'. The greater the tilt, the more pronounced is the difference between winter and summer.

These three cycles comprise what is often called the Milankovitch or Orbital Theory of climatic change. They have a temptingly close similarity in their periodicities to the durations of climatic change associated with the many glacials and interglacials of the last 1.6 million years. Indeed, they have been termed the 'pacemaker of the ice ages'.

Once the incoming solar radiation reaches the atmosphere, its passage to the surface of the earth is controlled by the gases, moisture and particulate matter that are present. Essential importance has been attached to the role of dust clouds emitted from volcanoes. These could increase the backscattering of incoming radiation and thus promote cooling. Volcanic dust veils produced by, for example, the eruption of Krakatoa in the 1880s and by Mount Pinatubo in 1991 caused global cooling for a matter of a few years. However, changing levels of volcanic activity are not the only way in which changes in atmosphere transparency might occur. For example, dust can be emplaced into the atmosphere by the wind erosion of fine-grained sediment and soil, and we know from the extensive deposits of wind-laid silts (loess) of glacial age that during the glacial maxima the atmosphere was probably very dusty, contributing to global cooling.

Carbon dioxide, methane, nitrous oxide, sulphur dioxide and water vapour can also modify the receipt of solar radiation. Particular attention has focused in recent years on the role of carbon dioxide (CO_2) in the atmosphere. This gas is virtually transparent to incoming solar radiation but absorbs outgoing terrestrial infra-red radiation – radiation that would otherwise escape to space and result in heat loss from the lower atmosphere. In general, through the mechanism of this so-called greenhouse effect, low levels of CO_2 in the atmosphere would be expected to lead to cooling, and high levels would be expected to produce a 'heat trap'. The same applies to levels of methane and nitrous oxide, which, molecule for molecule, are even more effective greenhouse gases than CO_2. Recently it has proved possible to retrieve CO_2 from gas bubbles preserved in layers of ice in deep-ice cores drilled from the polar regions. Analyses of changes in CO_2 concentrations in these cores have provided truly remarkable results and have demonstrated that CO_2 changes and climatic changes have progressed in approximate synchroneity over the last 160,000 years. Thus the last interglacial around 120,000 years ago was a time of high CO_2 levels, the last glacial maximum around 18,000 years ago of low CO_2 levels, and the early Holocene a time of very rapid rise in CO_2 levels. The reasons for the observed natural change in greenhouse gas concentrations are still the subject of active scientific research.

Once incoming radiation from the sun reaches the earth's surface it may be absorbed or reflected according to the nature of the surface, and in particular according to whether it is land or water, covered in dark vegetation or desert, and whether it is mantled by snow.

The effect of the received radiation on climate also depends on the distribution and altitude of land masses and oceans. These too are subject to change in a wide variety of ways – the plates that comprise the earth's crust are ever moving, mountain belts may grow or subside, and oceans and straits open and close. These processes shift areas into new latitudes, transform the world's wind belts and modify the climatically very important ocean currents.

In this discussion of causes it is also crucial to consider feedbacks. Such feedbacks are responses to the original forcing factors that act either to increase and intensify the original forcing (this we call positive feedback) or to decrease or reverse it (negative feedback). Clouds, ice and snow, and water vapour are three of the most important feedback mechanisms. An example of a positive feedback is the role of snow. Under cold conditions this falls rather than rain, it changes the albedo (reflectivity) of the ground surface and causes further cooling of the air above it. Similarly water vapour is a major greenhouse gas and a warmer climate produces more water vapour. This is because the rate of evaporation from the oceans and the water-holding capacity of the air would both increase as temperatures rise.

Finally, it may well be that the atmosphere and the oceans possess a degree of internal instability which furnishes a built-in mechanism of change so that some small and random change might, through the operation of positive feedbacks and the passage of thresholds, have extensive and long-term effects. Small triggers might have big consequences.

The presence of humans on the face of the earth will not cause all these natural mechanisms to cease abruptly. The next big question is, however, which of these mechanisms might be affected by human deeds?

Humans and the Climate Machine

While humans are at present incapable of modifying some of these natural mechanisms of climate change – the output of solar radiation, the presence of fine interstellar matter, the earth's variations, volcanic eruptions, mountain building and the overall pattern of land masses and oceans – there are some key areas where humans may be capable of making significant changes to global climates. The most important categories of influence are in terms of the chemical composition of the atmospheric gases, the particulates in the atmosphere and the albedo of the earth's surface.

Since the beginning of the Industrial Revolution some 300 or so years ago, humans have been taking stored carbon out of the earth in the form of fossil fuels – coal, oil and natural gas – and burning it to make carbon dioxide (CO_2), heat, water vapour and smaller amounts of sulphur dioxide, methane and other gases. Another factor that may make a substantial contribution to global carbon dioxide levels, which have risen from around 280 ppm (parts per million) by volume in pre-industrial times to over 360 ppm by volume today, is the burning of forests and changes in the organic contents of soils that are subjected to deforestation and cultivation.

Global emissions of carbon dioxide from fossil fuel burning have climbed since 1950 from 1,620 million tons of carbon to 6,056 million tons of carbon in 1995. The United States, at 1,400 million tons, was the largest source of carbon emissions in 1995, and it also had the highest per capita emissions: 5–25 tons of carbon annually. Its per capita emissions were more than seven times of those of China, twenty-five times of those of India. However, China, with its heavy reliance on coal, its inefficient use of energy and its burgeoning energy demand, could, before long, surpass the USA as a carbon emitter. Between 1990 and 1994 China's emissions went up by 13 per cent.

Because of the greenhouse mechanism one would expect increased CO_2 levels in the atmosphere to lead to an increase in surface temperatures.

In addition to making CO_2 levels build up in the atmosphere, humans are enhancing the greenhouse effect by causing the levels of some other greenhouse gases to increase. Individually their concentrations and effects may appear minor, but as a group they may be major, for individually some of them are much more effective, molecule for molecule, than CO_2. One of the more important of such trace gases is methane, levels of which have gone up about 2.5 times over natural background levels. This increase results primarily from increased rice cultivation in methane-generating water-logged paddy fields, the growing numbers of flatulent and belching domestic cattle, waste disposal and the burning of fossil fuels. Man-made chlorofluorocarbon (CFC) emissions have also increased and not only attack the ozone layer, but also have a disproportionately high greenhouse potential. Nitrous oxide (N_2O) can also contribute to the greenhouse effect. The combustion of fossil fuels, the use of ammonia-based synthetic fertilizers, deforestation and biomass burning are among those processes that can cause its concentration in the atmosphere to rise. Other trace gases that could play a greenhouse role include bromide compounds, carbon tetrafluoride, carbon tetrachloride and methyl chloride.

A combination of industrial and agricultural activities is also leading to changes in the small-particulate (aerosol) content of the atmosphere. Industrial pollution and desertification can cause the atmosphere to become more turbid and this in turn can lower temperatures, suppress convectional activity and change the availability of nuclei for cloud condensation and rain formation. In recent years there has been particular interest in the possibility that sulphate aerosols derived primarily from the burning of fossil fuels could absorb and reflect solar radiation and modify clouds. This would significantly decrease the input of incoming radiation from the sun and, in contrast to the greenhouse effect, exert a cooling influence on the planet. However, the most catastrophic effects of anthropogenic aerosols could be those resulting from a nuclear war. Explosion, fire and wind might generate a great pall of smoke and dust which would make the world hellishly dark and bitterly cold. It has been estimated that, if the exchange reached a level of several thousand megatons, a 'nuclear winter' would occur in which temperatures over much of the world would be depressed to well below freezing point.

Fears were also expressed that as a result of the smoke palls generated by the Gulf War in 1991 there might be severe climatic impacts. Studies have suggested that because most of the smoke generated by the oilwell fires stayed in the lower troposphere and had only a short residence time in the air, the effects were local (some cooling) rather than global, and that the operation of the South Asian monsoon was not affected to any significant degree.

Another major possible cause of anthropogenic climate change is that achieved by changing the albedo of the ground surface and the extent to which the surface reflects incoming solar radiation. Land-use and land-cover changes create differences in albedo which have important effects on the energy balance of an area. For instance, tall rainforest may have an albedo as low as 9 per cent, while the albedo of a desert may be as high as 37 per cent. Ground deprived of a vegetation cover as a result of deforestation and over-grazing (as in parts of the Sahel) has a very much higher albedo than ground covered in plants. This could affect temperature levels.

Likewise, deforestation in Amazonia would, through the effects of changes in surface roughness and albedo, lead to reductions in both precipitation and evaporation. The surface roughness effect occurs because rainforest has quite a jagged canopy, and this in turn affects wind flow. Moreover, if humid tropical rainforests are cut down, the amount of moisture transpired into the atmosphere above them will be reduced, thereby diminishing the potential for rain. The spread of irrigation, conversely, could lead to increased atmospheric humidity levels in the world's drylands. The High Plains of the USA, for example, are normally covered with sparse grasses and have dry soils throughout the summer; evapotranspiration there is very low. In the last four decades, however, irrigation has been developed throughout large parts of the area, greatly increasing summer evapotranspiration levels. There is some strong statistical evidence of warm season rainfall enhancement through irrigation in parts of this area.

There are some other more minor ways in which we could have an impact on the climate system, namely by changing the state of the oceans. It is possible, for example, to change the ice cover, salinity and currents of the Arctic Ocean by diverting freshwater from major rivers and it is theoretically possible to dam some of the world's narrower straits.

However, whether one is dealing with natural or anthropogenic causes of climate change, establishing causation is a devilish business characterized by an exceptional degree of intellectual instability and controversy. As the geographer William Meyer expressed it:

In climatology, the distance in space and time between causes and effects and their connection through a web or loop of invisible mechanisms pose particularly formidable obstacles to fitting the pieces of the puzzle together, or rather to solving what is less a jigsaw than a connect-the-dots puzzle. Lines can be drawn from a wide range of events regarded as possible effects, to produce any number of plausible patterns, yet only a few of which can be correct.

We also find it difficult to know whether the warming trend of the last hundred years can be attributed to an enhanced greenhouse effect. The spasmodic character of the observed warming, with a long standstill between 1940 and 1975, is difficult to explain and it will be many years before any clear signal of greenhouse global warming emerges from the year-to-year noise with sufficient clarity to silence those with doubts. Opponents of the theory of the enhanced greenhouse effect point to the fact that at least half of the warming that has taken place over the last hundred years occurred before two-thirds of the enhancement of the major greenhouse gases took place. They also point to the fact that, while general circulation models (GCMs – see next section) predict that the southern hemisphere should warm least and slowest, it in reality has shown a more greenhouse-like pattern than the northern hemisphere.

Can We Predict Future Climates?

Given the multitude of forcing factors and feedbacks and the complex links between air, water, land and the organic world, an immediate reaction to the question 'Can we predict future climates?' would be 'No'. Certainly in a whole variety of ways our predictive skills are both blunt and naive, but the implications of even quite modest climate changes are so profound for so many aspects of human existence that we have to grapple with the problem and develop our capabilities. This is precisely what that great co-operative endeavour, the Intergovernmental Panel on Climate Change (IPCC), has been doing since it was established in 1988. Let us now consider the methodologies that they have developed, for they have concerted the efforts of a large number of the world's most able climatologists.

The main means of projecting future climates are climate models called general circulation models (GCMs). They are based upon physical laws that describe the atmospheric and oceanic dynamics and physics, and upon empirical relationships, and their depiction as mathematical equations. These equations are solved numerically using large computers. The main uncertainties in simulations using GCMs arise from problems of adequately representing clouds and their radiative properties, the coupling between the atmosphere and the oceans, and the detailed processes that operate at the land surface. Like all models they involve a range of assumptions and they remain relatively coarse in scale. It is not surprising perhaps that different GCMs give quite different projections.

Further uncertainties are presented by the possibility of non-linear responses and by surprises. Unexpected external influences, such as a volcanic eruption, might lead to unexpected and relatively rapid or sudden shifts in the climate system. Some scientists also worry that the ocean could be modified were the west Antarctic ice sheet to surge or collapse into the Southern Ocean.

We also need to be mindful of the problems presented by complex feedbacks. For example, terrestrial ecosystems and climate are closely coupled so that, although climate change will have an impact on vegetation cover, soils and the like, changes in the character of terrestrial ecosystems will influence the climate system and alter thereby the release or storage of gases like CO_2, methane and nitrous oxide. Likewise a change of climate could change the nature of ocean salinity, ocean currents and water density, triggering a change in the whole oceanic circulation which could in turn alter the climate system. Some scientists argue that greenhouse heating may lead to the formation of more clouds, shielding the earth's surface and cooling the planet. This increase in cloud cover would be an example of potential negative feedback.

Our knowledge of certain crucial components of the atmospheric system may be rudimentary. This is, for example, a particular concern with regard to the potential role that sulphate aerosols might play in global cooling. Consider the use of the word 'uncertainty' in this context in the latest IPCC report (my italics):

> The direct radiative cooling effect of tropospheric aerosols is estimated to be about 20% of the direct radiative heating effect of greenhouse gases, with a factor of two *uncertainty*; the indirect effect, via the effect of aerosol on cloud properties, is much more *uncertain*. Thus the *uncertainty* in aerosol radiative forcing is the largest source of *uncertainty* in the total radiative forcing of climate over the past industrial period.

What levels of greenhouse gases and aerosols are going to accumulate in the atmosphere? This is another area where a large amount of speculation is involved. How is the world economy going to evolve? Will China develop its huge resources of poor-quality carbon-emitting coal? Will nuclear power make a comeback? How fast will land-cover changes, including tropical deforestation, proceed in coming decades? Will national and international action be effective in slowing down emissions of greenhouse gases? We can only guess.

Another source of uncertainty is precisely what will

happen to all the gases we are emitting. How much is going to be absorbed in particular by the oceans and by vegetation? Our knowledge on these matters is still imperfect.

The IPCC 1996 report gives us the best available indication of how climate may change between now and 2100. Bearing in mind the warming effect of green-house gases and the cooling effect of sulphate aerosols the IPCC projects that temperatures will on average rise between 1°C and 3.5°C. The warming will vary in its degree in different parts of the world, with the maximum warming taking place over land in high northern latitudes. Some regions, for example China, could actually become cooler.

Precipitation amounts show a very complex projection of change. Precipitation is expected to go up on a global basis. It is also expected to increase in high latitudes in winter and in most cases the increases will extend well into mid-latitudes. There is little agreement as to what will happen in the tropics.

A general warming would tend to lead to an increase in extremely high temperature events (which could create health and comfort problems) and a decrease in winter days with extremely low temperatures. It might also magnify the probability of intense precipitation, though there is no agreement as to whether or not the frequency and intensity of tropical hurricanes would change.

This summary of the IPCC findings indicates that

there are still reservations and uncertainties, and that the degree of change that can be anticipated is less than has often been postulated in the past. Bearing these points in mind, is there cause for concern?

Climatic Impacts

Although the amounts of change that are predicted may at first sight appear low in quantity and far off in time, they are in terms of natural environments substantial and rapid. Let me extract some of the more thought-provoking comments of the IPCC's 1996 report. On forests:

> a substantial fraction (a global average of one-third, varying by region from one-seventh to two-thirds) of the existing forested area of the world will undergo major changes in broad vegetation types ... climate change is expected to occur at a rapid rate relative to the speed at which forest species grow, reproduce and establish themselves ... the species composition of forests is likely to change; entire forest types may disappear.

On deserts and desertification: 'Deserts are likely to become more extreme – in that, with few exceptions, they are projected to become hotter but not significantly wetter.' On the cryosphere: 'Between one-third and one-half of existing mountain glacier mass could disappear over the next 100 years.' On mountain regions:

The projected decrease in the extent of mountain glaciers, permafrost and snow cover caused by a warmer climate will affect hydrologic systems, soil stability and related socio-economic systems ... Recreational industries – of increasing economic importance to many regions – are also likely to be disrupted.

On coastal systems:

Climate change and a rise in sea level or changes in storm surges could result in the erosion of shores and associated habitat, increased salinity of estuaries and freshwater aquifers, altered tidal ranges in rivers and bays, changes in sediment and nutrient transport, a change in the pattern of chemical and microbiological contamination in coastal areas, and increased coastal flooding. Some coastal ecosystems are particularly at risk, including saltwater marshes, mangrove ecosystems, coastal wetlands, coral reefs, coral atolls, and river deltas.

Some landscape types will be highly sensitive to global warming. This may be the case because they are located in zones where it is forecast that climate will change to an above average degree. This applies, for instance, in the high latitudes of North America and Eurasia, where the degree of warming may be three or four times greater than the presumed global average. It may also be the case for some critical areas where particularly substantial changes in rainfall may result from global warming. For example, various methods of climatic prediction produce scenarios in which the American High Plains will become considerably drier. Other landscapes will be highly sensitive because certain landscape forming processes are very closely controlled by climatic conditions. If such landscapes are close to particular climatic thresholds then quite modest amounts of climatic change can switch them from one state to another.

High-latitude tundra terrains may be regarded as especially sensitive. As already noted, they are likely to undergo exceptionally substantial temperature change. In addition, permafrost, which underlies large tracts, is one of those phenomena which is most closely controlled by temperature. This is because by definition it cannot occur where mean annual temperatures are above the freezing point for water and the latitudinal limits of different types of permafrost can be related to varying degrees of negative temperature. Thus the equatorward limit of continuous permafrost may approximate to the −5°C isotherm while the equatorward limit of discontinuous or sporadic permafrost may approximate to the −2°C isotherm. It is likely that the permafrost will be displaced polewards by 100 to 250 kilometres for every 1°C rise in mean annual temperature. Its most rapid melting would occur in those terrain types underlain by surface materials with low ice contents, and the slowest response would be in ice-rich materials, which require more heat to thaw. The presence of thick, organic layers (e.g. peat) might also buffer the effects of increased surface temperatures in some areas by providing a degree of insulation.

There is historical evidence that permafrost can degrade speedily. For instance, during the warm optimum of the Holocene (*c.* 6,000 years ago) the southern limits of discontinuous permafrost in the Russian Arctic were up to 600 kilometres north of their present position. Similarly, during the warming phase that has characterized recent decades, it has been demonstrated that along the Mackenzie Highway in Canada the southern fringe of the discontinuous permafrost zone has moved north by about 120 kilometres between 1962 and 1988, in response to an increase over the same period of 1°C in mean annual temperature.

In areas where rapid permafrost decay occurs, the consequences will be legion. They include ground subsidence, increased erosion of coastlines and river banks, and an increase in landslide activity and other types of slope instability. Many engineering structures could be put at risk.

Given the rates of glacier retreat experienced in many mountainous areas in response to the warming episode since the 1880s, it is also probable that many glaciers will shrink or even disappear altogether in the future. Many of them have certainly shrunk in both length and volume since the demise of the Little Ice Age, though the rate has not been constant nor the process uninterrupted. In general terms, however, alpine glaciers can retreat up their valleys at rates of 20–70 metres per year over extended periods of some decades. Glaciers from areas as diverse as the Highlands of East Africa or the Southern Alps of New Zealand are likely to shrivel or disappear. This in turn has implications for water supply, irrigation and hydroelectricity generation.

The world's desert margins are also highly sensitive. Repeatedly throughout the Holocene their dune fields and sand seas have flipped from a state of vegetated stability to states of drought-induced surface instability. It is only with the recent availability of the new techniques of thermoluminescent and optical dating that this sensitivity to quite minor climatic perturbations has become evident. Geomorphologists, using the output from GCMs, combined with an index of dune mobility which incorporates wind strength and the ratio of mean annual rainfall to moisture loss by evapotranspiration, have shown that, with global warming, sand dunes and sand sheets on the Great Plains are likely to become reactivated over a significant part of the region, particularly if the frequencies of wind speeds above the crucial threshold speed for sand movement were to increase to even a moderate degree. The same applies to dust-storm activity in the cereal-producing lands of the Great Plains and the Canadian Prairies, where the application of GCMs shows that conditions comparable to the devastating Dust Bowl years of the 1930s are likely to be experienced once again.

Another sensitive environmental type may be the

coral reef, for increased sea-surface temperatures could have adverse consequences for corals which are near the maximum limits of their thermal tolerance. Most coral species cannot tolerate temperatures greater than about 30°C, and even a rise in seawater temperature of 1–2°C could adversely affect many shallow-water coral species. Indeed, increased temperatures have been identified as a cause of widespread coral bleaching (loss of symbiotic zooxanthellae). In recent years various studies suggest that coral bleaching was a widespread feature in the warm years of the 1980s. Those corals already stressed by high temperatures or by marine pollution might well find it less easy to cope with rapidly rising sea levels than would more healthy coral. Moreover, it is possible that increased ultra-violet radiation resulting from ozone-layer depletion could aggravate bleaching and mortality caused by global warming.

Indeed, T. J. Goreau and R. L. Hayes have produced maps of global coral-bleaching episodes between 1983 and 1991 and have related them to maps of sea-surface temperatures over that period. They find that areas of severe bleaching are related to what they describe as ocean 'hot spots' where marked above-average temperature anomalies exist. They argue that coral reefs are ecosystems that may be uniquely prone to the effects of global warming.

If global warming continues almost all ecosystems can be replaced by migration of species from lower latitudes, except for the warmest ecosystems. These have no source of immigrants already adapted to warmer conditions. Their species must evolve new environmental tolerances if their descendants are to survive, a much slower process than migrations.

One aspect of sensitivity is what I have referred to elsewhere as the 'groggy earth' syndrome. Processes other than enhanced greenhouse warming, be they natural or anthropogenic, may render some environments particularly prone to the effects of warming. Global warming might compound the effects of processes already in operation. This can be illustrated by two examples of the effects of sea-level rise brought about by global warming. The first of these is the densely populated and intensively cultivated Nile Delta in Egypt. It is already suffering from severe erosion and salinity problems on its seaward margin. These are caused by the natural subsidence of the delta and by the way in which the sediment load entering the delta (which helps to build it up and out) has been diminished by the construction of that great sediment trap – the Aswan High Dam. Any accelerating global sea-level rise could only exacerbate the problem. A second example is provided by some of the world's coastal mega-cities and conurbations. Many of them, including Tokyo, Bangkok and Venice, are already susceptible to severe flooding, not only because they are low-lying, but because they are sinking as a result of overpumping of groundwater. Again, any further rise in sea level could only compound their problems.

Once again, however, there are those who would doubt whether the impacts of the enhanced greenhouse effects on ecosystems will inevitably be detrimental. For example, some argue that increased levels of atmospheric CO_2 would be a positive boon, especially for plants and crops. Sherwood Idso has repeatedly suggested that enriching the air with CO_2 helps plants grow better because carbon dioxide is the primary raw material used by plants to produce food by the process of photosynthesis. Another way it enhances growth is by stimulating plants to reduce the size of the pores in their leaves through which water is evaporated and lost to the atmosphere. Indeed he argues that plants that barely manage to subsist on the borders of barren deserts will benefit very substantially.

The Intergovernmental Panel on Climate Change also provides an analysis of some of the more direct implications of climate change for a range of human activities.

If one considers agriculture, climatic change will have direct effects through changes in temperature, water balance, atmospheric composition and extreme events. There will also be indirect effects through changes in the distribution, frequency and severity of pest and disease outbreaks, fire, weed infestations or changes in soil properties. Various analyses suggest that lower latitudes will have to withstand more negative consequences of climate change than will temperate areas. The significance of this is that these are the locations of many of the poorer and developing nations which are especially dependent on the agricultural sector for their survival.

The climatic sensitivity of some other sectors, such as industry, energy and transport, is relatively low compared to that of agriculture. However, the insurance sector may be greatly exercised by the consequences of extreme and unusual climatic events, which will make it difficult for insurance firms to adjust premiums appropriately. For example, were hurricanes to become more intense, frequent and geographically widespread, the implications could be extreme. Hurricane Andrew in Florida in 1992 led to insurance costs that amounted to $16.5 billion.

Human health is another area that could be adversely affected by climate changes. Direct health effects include heat-related conditions, particularly cardiorespiratory disease, while indirect effects include increases in the potential transmission of vector-borne infectious diseases such as malaria. Whereas 45 per cent of the world's human population presently lives in the climate zone where mosquitoes transmit malaria, models suggest that this proportion could increase to as much as 60 per cent by the latter half of the next century.

Reacting, Adapting and Mitigating

If, as the Intergovernmental Panel on Climate Change suggests, the enhanced greenhouse effect is likely to cause warming in the first century of the new millennium, what should we do? The IPCC itself summarized the options:

- implementing low-cost measures, such as energy efficiency, to reduce emissions of greenhouse gases;
- phasing out existing distortionary policies, such as some fossil-fuel subsidies, that reduce welfare and increase greenhouse-gas emissions directly or indirectly;
- switching from more to less carbon-intensive fuels or to carbon-free fuels to reduce emissions of greenhouse gases;
- enhancing or expanding greenhouse gas sinks or reservoirs, such as forests;
- implementing existing techniques (and developing new ones) for reducing methane and nitrous oxide emissions from industrial processes, landfills, agriculture, fossil-fuel extraction and transportion;
- instituting forms of international co-operation, such as joint implementation, technology transfer and tradable quotas to reduce the cost of limiting greenhouse gas emissions;

- planning and implementing measures to adapt to the consequences of climate change;
- undertaking additional research on climate-change causes, effects and adaptation (economic studies suggest that such research can yield high returns by reducing uncertainty about actions to address climate change);
- conducting techological research to enhance energy efficiency, minimize emissions of greenhouse gases from fossil-fuel use, and develop commercial non-fossil energy sources (in the long run, the cost and timing of availability of non-fossil energy technologies is one of the major determinants of the cost of addressing climate change);
- developing institutional mechanisms, such as insurance, to share the risks of damages due to climate change.

One area of considerable debate, however, has been how and when we should adapt to global warming. It is often said that there are two types of adaptation that may be necessary. The first of these types is reactive adaptation, whereby we adopt a wait-and-see attitude and respond to climatic change after it occurs. Alternatively, there is anticipatory adaptation, in which we take steps in advance of anticipated climate changes to minimize any potentially negative effects or to increase our ability to adapt to changes rapidly and inexpensively. In other words we hedge our bets.

Reactive adaptation may well be both feasible and effective. In many parts of the world we may find it possible to adapt to the most likely scenarios of future climatic change. We could, for instance, substitute heat- and drought-resistant crop varieties for those whose yields are reduced. Likewise, infrastructure, which is generally replaced on a much faster timescale than climatic change, could be modified to cope with changes in climate. It can also be argued that reactive adaptation is a strategy that does not involve spending money prematurely before some hypothetical changes occur.

On the other hand one can argue that a rapid climate change or significant increases in the frequency and intensity of extreme hazards such as floods, storms or droughts could make reactive adaptations more difficult and could create a threat for large numbers of people. Equally, some policies would have significant and tangible benefits even under current environmental conditions and would be valuable from a benefit/cost point of view even if no climatic change were to take place. These types of anticipatory policies are often called 'no-regrets policies' because they will succeed whether or not climatic change takes place, meaning that policy-makers should never have to regret their adoption. No-regrets policies may, nonetheless, be expensive, but we may get what is called a 'double benefit'. Thus if we slow the rate of deforestation in the humid tropics to decrease the rate of CO_2 emissions from biomass burning, we are also helping to preserve biodiversity. If we reduce CO_2 emissions through energy efficiency and conservation, we reduce other pollutants (for example, sulphur dioxide). If we succeed in reducing carbon dioxide emissions from traffic the policies that are likely to be used also reduce local pollution, noise, accidents and congestion. One could also, perhaps at no great cost, introduce planning controls to limit development in sensitive locations, such as highly populated, low-lying coastal plains.

A cogent reason that is given for taking action now, in spite of all the uncertainties, is that the timescale of atmospheric response is long. CO_2 that is being emitted into the atmosphere now will contribute to the increased concentration of this gas and the associated climate change for over a hundred years. Hence the more CO_2 that is emitted now, the more difficult it will prove to reduce the levels to those that will eventually be required. Moreover, the timescales for certain human responses can be long, as illustrated by the fact that the power stations that will produce our electric power three or four decades hence are being planned and built today.

According to what is called the Precautionary Principle we need to take out what is in effect an insurance policy against surprises and the unexpected. Even though the risk posed by such possibilities is impossible to assess and cannot therefore easily be quantified, it would not perhaps be prudent to ignore entirely unexpected possibilities in weighing the action that may be necessary.

It is also important for policymakers to have a clear view of the costs and benefits of global warming, for it is plainly crucial in determining whether it is worth spending large amounts of money to combat this potential threat. Environmental economists have been adressing this issue with vigour for some years. There are extreme difficulties in placing a value on such issues as biodiversity and amenity. Nonetheless some quantification of the costs of action against the likely costs of the consequences of inaction should at least be attempted.

The key need, if action is to be taken and to be effective, is to reduce emissions of greenhouse-enhancing gases. There are various means by which this might be achieved. First of all, it is possible to conserve energy and to use it more efficiently, by such means as insulating houses, designing domestic appliances that use less power and increasing the efficiency of coal-fired power stations and developing combined heat and power schemes. Likewise it is necessary to look at alternative means of power generation, including efficient gas-powered stations, nuclear stations and various types of renewable energy sources powered by sun, wind, water or biomass.

Some scientists have argued that the world's forests can make a contribution to the mitigation of global warming, either by reducing the rates of deforestation (especially in the tropics) or by active afforestation. Both processes would help to store carbon rather than releasing it into the atmosphere. Similarly, methane emissions could be minimized by reducing biomass burning associated with deforestation, by recycling waste or using gas generated from waste for energy production, and by reducing leakage from natural gas pipelines.

Another method that has been proposed to control CO_2 emissions is a system of 'joint implementation schemes', 'carbon offsets' or 'tradable emissions permits'. The idea behind this is that countries which find they have high abatement costs could be credited for cheaper abatement efforts undertaken in other countries. For example, an industrialized country might choose to plant forests (and so sequestrate carbon) in a developing country.

One can also ask whether we have a clear picture, if we wish to apportion blame and to charge the polluter, about national carbon dioxide inventories. Do we charge polluters for their past emissions or their present emissions? Should we tax an Asian peasant whose buffalo and paddy field emit methane in the way we might tax a California adolescent who owns a large dune buggy that emits carbon dioxide?

Since the Industrial Revolution, industrialized countries have 'used up' more than their fair share of the atmospheric resource, causing cumulative pollution. In other words it can be argued that industrialized countries have already incurred a large debt and should accordingly be allowed smaller future emission levels.

They have become richer in part because they have used up a disproportionate amount of the atmospheric resource and should thus compensate the poor by allowing them larger future emission levels. On the other hand, should the 'sins' of fathers be visited on their sons?

The concept of introducing a carbon tax to reduce CO_2 emissions, although seemingly simple, has not been universally welcomed. It has been argued that unless the tax were large it would be ineffective but that if it were large it would be politically unacceptable. Moreover, since a carbon tax is unlikely to be introduced by all countries, energy-intense industries might switch to those countries which did not introduce a tax. Indeed, given that many European countries are already very energy efficient, it is conceivable that any shift of production to less energy-efficient parts of the world could actually raise rather than depress global CO_2 emissions. This effect is sometimes called 'carbon leakage'.

There are also various problems with the costs of strategies to reduce emissions. It is agreed that any draconian measures could retard economic development. Moreover, the countries that can afford to combat greenhouse warming will not be the main beneficiaries of abatement policies. It is those countries potentially most at risk from the effects of global warming and sea-level rise, such as Bangladesh, that can least afford to divert resources from their own development.

It is a moot question whether the world's greatest producer of carbon-dioxide emissions, the United States of America, would wish to spend money now to benefit other countries that might suffer from global warming in the future.

Linked with this is the question of whether the developed countries that have achieved a high level of economic development through the lavish use of fossil-fuel resources could expect the less developed and poor nations of the world to limit their use of fossil fuels and their rate of economic advancement. Similarly, can countries that have already cut down most of their own forests, such as Britain, argue with any great authority that developing countries should not follow their example?

So, then, there are controversies about whether anticipatory adaptation is desirable in itself and about the feasibility of the various methods that might be employed were it to prove acceptable. If the majority of governments in the world (and individuals) take anticipatory adaptation seriously, there is some prospect that rates of global warming could at least be slowed down. It is, however, by no means certain that this will prove to be the case. A combination of prevailing short-termism, cheerful optimism and climatological cynicism may defeat the efforts of those who see the wisdom of no-regrets policies.

Beyond Global Warming

As I have stressed repeatedly in this essay, accelerated global warming may never occur and naturally operating climatic processes may continue to cause climate to change. Indeed, in the longer term – that is over the next few thousands of years rather than over the next century or so – it is not inconceivable that the world will be subjected to the chilling prospect of global cooling. It is salutary to remember that in the 1970s academics and scientific journalists were warning us repeatedly and with cogency that the ice age was coming. They did so for reasons that are still largely tenable.

First of all, the 1960s and 1970s were a time of remarkable developments in the study of past climates. The increasing availability of a range of relatively accurate dating techniques enabled palaeoclimatologists to obtain a clear idea of the timing of past events over hundreds of thousands of years. Secondly, because of development in boring and coring technology the retrieval of long sequences of environmental information could be achieved by recovering long cores of sediment from the ocean floor. This provided a longer and less broken sequence than could be obtained over most parts of the land surface, where erosion could have created gaps in the record. Cores were also retrieved from the great ice caps, and from the floors of large lakes, while the great sheets of loess also provided long-term sequences of sediment.

The combination of dates and a long-term unbroken sedimentary record enabled scientists to construct, for the first time, a relatively clear, accurate and lengthy picture of environmental changes over the last few millions of years. Scientists spoke with excitement of the 'Pleistocene Revolution' for the transformation of our views about the pattern, progress and causes of climatic variability.

Their findings had a range of implications for climatic prediction. One of these findings was that the world's climate system had flipped repeatedly in an almost cyclic manner for some hundreds of thousands of years, alternating between glacials and interglacials. The implication of this is that if the cause of this cyclicity could be established, then the mechanism would be predictable and so would the climate changes that would ensue.

Secondly, such a cyclic mechanism, orbital forcing (see pp. 13–14), was found, and its periodicity tied in well with the observed periodicities in the palaeoclimatic record from the ocean floors. Just as orbital forcing can be predicted, so can the climatic changes which it will drive in the future.

Thirdly, it was apparent from the palaeoclimatic record that interglacial conditions of the type which we experience today (and have experienced over the 10,000 or so years of the Holocene) are relatively short-lived and atypical in the longer term. Cold, rather than warmth, has been the norm over hundreds of thousands of years.

Fourthly, palaeoclimatologists came to realize that the onset of climatic changes could be more sudden and rapid than had previously been thought. A mechanism called 'instantaneous glacierization' or 'snowblitz' was advanced to explain how it was that great ice sheets, rather than trundling and creeping slowly sideways from higher latitudes to lower, could build up rapidly in places. A spate of scary, paperback novels based on snowblitz appeared at airport bookstalls, their covers emblazoned with pictures of walls of ice enveloping the skyscrapers of Manhattan. The science journalist Nigel Calder described snowblitz thus in *The Weather Machine* (1974):

> the ice sheet comes out of the sky and grows, not sideways, but from the bottom upwards. Like airborne troops, invading snowflakes seize whole countries in a single winter. The fact that they have come to stay does not become apparent, though, until the following summer. Then the snow that piled up on the meadow fails to melt completely. Instead it lies though the summer and autumn, reflecting the sunshine. It chills the air and guarantees more snow next winter. Thereafter, as fast as the snow can fall, the ice sheet gradually grows thicker over a huge area.

Fifthly, the high-resolution palaeoclimatic record in polar ice cores and deep peat bogs in Europe indicated that the onset of past changes had sometimes indeed been very rapid and that climates had flipped from one state to another.

This trend towards a catastrophic view of the onset of an ice age makes a very big difference to any estimate of the possibility of a drastic change of climate occurring in the relatively near future. Indeed Calder went on: 'The ice age could in principle start next summer, or at any rate during the next hundred years, with a ferocity that could not be mistaken for a "mere" climatic fluctuation like the Little Ice Age.'

More recently further research has been done into the timing, degree and course of abrupt climatic changes. In particular the climatic record from immensely long ice cores from Greenland has given an indication that changes have on occasions taken place with remarkable suddenness. Such sudden changes, if they could take place in the past, might also occur in the future.

Consider, for example, the role of a catastrophic volcanic eruption. Such an event could theoretically occur at any time. One such event took place in Sumatra 73,000 years ago. It was called the Toba super-eruption. One can gauge its power by comparing the amount of aerosols (dust and clouds) that it spewed into the atmosphere with recent severe eruptions. It produced around 1000 Tg (1×10^{12} grams) of SO_2 aerosols. The

Mount Pinatubo eruption of 1991 produced 30 Tg and the eruption of Krakatoa in 1883 produced about 50 Tg. The duration of the Toba event was up to two weeks, and ash was deposited over large tracts of the Indian Ocean. The clouds of aerosols went 27 to 37 kilometres into the air, and the low-latitude position of Toba probably led to an efficient injection of material into the stratosphere in both hemispheres.

Climatologists consider that the increased atmospheric opacity that it caused resulted in a 'volcanic winter', so that global surface temperatures decreased by as much as 3–5°C for a few years. It is possible that snow cover and sea-ice extents increased at sensitive northern latitudes, triggering the main northern-hemisphere transition from warmth to cold at the start of the last glacial cycle. This change has been dated to around the time of the eruption.

Conclusion

The world's climate has always been changing and will always be changing. It changed before humans evolved on the face of the earth, it has provided a shifting backdrop during the time that humans have been inhabitants of the earth, and now, for the first time, humans may be starting to modify that backdrop themselves. The human race is embarking on a great chemistry experiment which many scientists believe poses a threat both to ecosystems and to humans themselves. Predictions of the degree, spread and consequences of this experiment are bedevilled by uncertainties, as is the will of people and politicians to take steps that might delay, reduce or even reverse the process of change. Nonetheless, powerful though humankind may have become, nature is still more powerful, incomprehensible and potentially capricious. Global warming, because of the enhanced greenhouse effect, may become a reality over coming decades, but in the longer term global cooling may be a more likely future.

The 'mere' Little Ice Age, to which Calder referred, was a time of considerable social, economic and political difficulties for the inhabitants of north-western Europe, but a full-blown ice age would transform the world and make large tracts of it totally uninhabitable. Ice sheets would lead to the complete or almost complete obliteration of all of North America down to the Ohio–Mississippi basin, Scandinavia, Switzerland and the British Isles. If one had to make a choice between modest global warming or the sudden onset of an ice age one would, undoubtedly, settle for the former.

Further Reading

A. S. Goudie, *The Human Impact on the Natural Environment* (4th edition), Oxford, 1993.

A. S. Goudie, *Environmental Change* (3rd edition), Oxford, 1993.

T. E. Graedel and P. J. Caruzen, *Atmosphere, Climate and Change*, New York, 1995.

D. Eisma (ed.), *Climate Change, Impact on Coastal Habitation*, Boca Raton, 1995.

D. D. Kemp, *Global Environmental Issues: a Climatological Approach* (2nd edition), London, 1994.

J. T. Houghton, *Global Warming: The Complete Briefing*, Oxford, 1994.

J. T. Houghton, L. G. Meira Filho, B. A. Callander, N. Harris, A. Kaltenberg and K. Maskell (ed.), *The Science of Climate Change*, Cambridge, 1995.

J. Leggett, *Climate Change and the Financial Sector*, Munich, 1996.

PREDICTIONS